Thom Tammaro

When the Italians Came to My Home Town

When the Italians Came
to My Home Town

Poems
and an Essay by

~~Thom Tammaro~~

Thom Tammaro

for my friends at CASA — Saluti!

October 5, 1997

SPOON RIVER POETRY PRESS
1995

Publication of this book is supported by a grant from the Southwest Minnesota Arts and Humanities Council. Our many thanks.

Published by Spoon River Poetry Press, David R. Pichaske, editor, P.O. Box 6, Granite Falls, Minnesota 56241.

Printed by Thomson and Shore, Dexter, Michigan.

Cover Photograph by Walker Evans: "Graveyard, Houses, and Steel Mill: Bethlehem, Pennsylvania, November, 1935," LC-USF342-1167A, used with the kind permission of the Library of Congress.

Photo of Thom Tammaro by Anne Lennox, Moorhead, Minnesota, used by permission.

Interior photo (page 34) "St. Agatha Grotto," by Thom Tammaro.

ISBN: 0-944024-28-9

1 2 3 4 5   95 96 97 98 99

When the Italians Came
to My Home Town

"This too is true: stories can save us."
—Tim O'Brien: "The Lives of the Dead"

for Sheila, la bella figura

CONTENTS

I.

II. Intermezzo

III.

I

"Oh childhood, what was us going away,
going where? Where?"

—Rilke, "Childhood"

INNOCENT TRAVELER

There was a great storm in the mountains of central Italy that night. Thunder shook the ground, trees trembled, lightening lit up the sky. Rain fell, unrelenting, for hours, making the steep paths slippery and treacherous. In a farmhouse high above the village, a young woman begged her father and mother to offer her suitor the barn for the night. Reluctantly, they agreed and the young man covered himself in straw, slept dry and safe among barn animals, until morning light.

Coming down the mountain path the next morning, the young man came upon a circle of villagers huddled around the stiff, soaked corpse of a young man. Fingers pointed to bullet holes, one in the side of his head and another just above the heart. The dead man's eyes were wide open until someone forced their lids closed for the last time. Later, the murderer was arrested and confessed to the killing, but said the bullets were meant for the young man who courted the woman who lived in the farmhouse high above the village. Two days later the campanile bells echoed above the village where peasants mourned the tragedy of the innocent traveler.

A few years later, the young man and woman were married, and shortly thereafter boarded a ship in Naples and sailed to America. This was 1907. Their youngest daughter was born in 1924, and nine years later the mother died from a brain tumor. And sometime later I became the second child of the youngest daughter and her husband.

This afternoon, coming home through the rain, I remember this story and feel the sanctity of my life. How our coming into this world is precarious, our stay tenuous, our going definite. And so I thank the rain. And I thank the barn animals and the straw that kept my grandfather warm and dry through the night. I am even moved to thank the desperate lover and his jealousy. But most of all I thank the innocent traveler coming down the mountain path in the dark, stepping into my life, unaware of what lay ahead in unrelenting rain.

FEBRUARY, 1951

In the cold middle of the month, in the late gray sky afternoon, a young man, six years from the war and four years from his wedding, steps from the mill gate, which he will enter and exit for the next thirty-one years of his working life, onto the frozen bricks of Factory Avenue. A gust of winter wind whips his 6' 1" slender frame, sending flakes from a patch of new snow swirling around his body. Turning up the collar of his olive-drab fatigue field coat which he will wear well beyond middle age, he heads home, alone in the last light which has given in to steel-gray clouds drifting across what is left of that Pennsylvania day.

A mile away a young wife, four years from her wedding, beautiful in her thick Jane Russell hair and robust in her life, waits for him as she will do every day—or night when he works the night shift—for the next thirty-one years. She is wearing a long sleeve blue cotton print dress that her sister gave her and a black wool button down sweater with pearl buttons that she received as a gift from him last Christmas. Coffee perks in a small tin pot with a broken glass stopper as it will for the next thirty-one years. She wipes a swirl of snow from the window pane and looks for his slender shadow coming up the street. She opens the door to a blast of winter air when she hears him step from the dirt path to the wooden porch and climb the steps to the front door. When they see each other they smile as they will for the next thirty-one years. He walks through, one hand clasping shut the collar of his fatigue field coat, the other wrapped around the handle of the black metal lunch pail which he will carry to and from work for the next thirty-one years. They pause, embrace: she reaching her arms around his shoulders and standing tip-toe to reach his lips; he bending down to meet her lips, letting go of his coat collar to wrap his free arm around her thin waist, drawing her to his body, the warm, black wool sweater pressing against the cold folds of his olive-drab coat. In the room above them, their first child, thin but never weak from a faulty heart, will sleep until nightfall. After they greet each other, he goes to the sink to wash away the day's work from his face and hands, then combs his brilliant black hair in a great sweep atop his head. They sit at the gray Formica table where they will eat their meals for the next thirty-one years, the yeasty smells of the kitchen all around them.

4

Below their second story flat above the butcher shop, swirls of snow sweep along the empty streets. And then in late afternoon darkness, without word, quick and deliberate as deer moving to water, they move to love each other. Somewhere deep inside their bodies they offer themselves, priest and priestess, in the holy sacrifice of their love, body and blood, flesh and bone, to the host I am to be, while the last flicker of February light finds its way down the long corridors of their love toward the first glimmer of my life—a distant planet orbiting in its path deep inside their bodies, waiting to take its place among the constellations. And then there was evening, and there was morning, and another day. And day after day, their creation filled the firmament, floating to find his place in this watery world.

ETERNITY

Take a tiny bird—say a wren or sparrow. Then take a mountain, as large as any in the world—say Everest. Think of that bird finding its way to the highest peak of that mountain once a year—say spring—for the sole purpose of sharpening its beak, which it does by drawing it back and forth across the craggy peak until the beak's edge is sharp as a surgeon's scalpel. Now when that mountain has worn down to the size of a pebble a child could hold in its palm—that, we were told, constitutes one second of eternity. And there are an infinite number of seconds in eternity, just as there are an infinite number of days in eternity. And remember: if you think you have found the largest number in the world, just add one to it. The same goes for eternity: if you think you know how many seconds or days there are in eternity, just add one. Now you begin to grasp eternity.

Now take a seven year old child, a second grader on the verge of receiving his First Communion, and tell him this story on the same afternoon the great concept of Sin is introduced and planted in his psyche. All done, of course, for the sake of illustrating to him how long he will have to spend in the afterlife in the bowels of Hell, should he choose the path of Sin. A path always paved, we know, by the consequences of choice. One always has choice, remember. One always chooses his own path to walk down.

Late one afternoon, you might find this boy walking home along his old neighborhood streets, gazing into the tree tops, scanning the telephone wires and roof tops, searching for the tiny bird whose trilling pierces the spring air. When the boy is deep into night's sleep, if you looked closely, you might notice how his lips flutter and tremble the way the thin tail feathers of a tiny bird flutter lighting out for its first journey and rendezvous with a mountain top. You might notice how the boy's lips open and a little cry comes forth, rushes against the night air, disappears, is lost in the darkness.

PRAYER FOR THE CONVERSION OF RUSSIA

Mary, hear our prayer:
Let us not hunger for the bread of this world,
But fill our hearts with the love of your joy!

That was the prayer we prayed in second grade, 1957, Purification of the Blessed Virgin Mary School, when we prayed mornings for the conversion of Russia. That was the year of atheists and Communists who, we were told, rode into the villages of starving Russian peasants and promised food if the villagers would give up God. Then later, as if to fulfill their promise, men riding atop truck loads of bread would drive through the village, tossing fresh loaves to the hungry— "Another village fallen to the Godless Russians," according to Sister Angelica. Sometime later during Religion lessons, when Sister read the story about the loaves and fishes, Bennie Capone raised his hand then asked if Jesus and the Apostles were Communists since they, too, delivered on their promise to feed the hungry. Later that week, Bennie was transferred to Father Pazzocane's class. The last I heard of Bennie Capone he had been arrested in Chicago in 1968 during the Democratic Convention.

The other reason we prayed for the conversion of Russia that year was the miracle at Fatima, Portugal, where one May day in 1917 three shepherd children saw the figure of a woman, brighter than the sun, standing on a cloud and floating above an evergreen tree. On the 13th of each month for six straight months they saw the same vision that no one else could see. Hearing of the story, thousands of villagers gathered in October, and while they fell to their knees claiming they saw movements in a tree and a great bright cloud arriving and departing, only the shepherd children—Lucia, Francesca and Jacinta—saw the vision of the bright woman. Later, the three children were kidnapped—probably by Communists Sister Angelica said—and were held for questioning for two days by the authorities. But four days later when the throng gathered again to witness the revelation of the bright woman, suddenly the sun rose at noon, trembled and rotated violently, then fell and danced above the heads of the terrified crowd. This "Miracle of the Sun" was repeated twice, and the woman of light revealed herself to the children as "Our Lady of the Rosary" and told them to pray for the conversion of Russia, that the rosary must be prayed during each second of each day, otherwise the world would cease spinning on its axis and come to a crashing end. As the story goes, before the bright woman departed she whispered the dates of World War III—the war that would end the world—to the children and told them that all mankind should pray for the conversion of Russia. Later Lucia agreed to write down the dates for Church officials, and these secrets, only known by the Popes, lie buried in a vault deep below the Vatican.

Back then, in the year of our obsession with Russia, rosaries and bread, we vowed never to tell anyone if we were hungry and to reject the promise and offer of bread from strangers who, after all, might be Communists working their secret plan. I thought of you last night, Bennie Capone, when I heard the evening news report that 100,000 pilgrims have made their way to a mountain top in Yugoslavia where the image of the Virgin has appeared to young people every evening since June of 1981, and that the faithful of Cleveland are flocking to an oil refinery along Lake Erie to witness "The Miracle of the Oil," where they say the silhouette of Christ can be seen in an oil splatter on the side of a storage tank.

Bennie Capone, you were right: hope is a passion sustained by hunger, bread, Russians, Sister Angelica, Father Pazzocane, rosaries. Who can blame the peasants for giving up the God who leaves them hungry? Who loves the hungry? The grief of empty stomachs? Who is feeding the hungry of Yugoslavia and Cleveland? Who are the fools and the fooled? Who sees the sun spinning above the treetops?

ST. PETER'S TEARS

After the betrayal, the story goes,
Peter followed Jesus to the High Priest's house
to learn more about the trial to come.
Peter lingered in the courtyard among
servants and soldiers, hoping to hear
word of Jesus' fate. When a maid asked
if he was one of the disciples, Peter said,
"Woman, I do not know him."

Later, servants and guards built
a fire in the courtyard and stood
around warming themselves in the cold
Jerusalem night. When Peter joined them,
a guard thought he recognized Peter
as one of the disciples. But again,
Peter said, "Man, I don't know him."

Toward dawn, a cousin of the guard
whose ear Peter cut off the night before
recognized Peter and asked,
"Did I see you in the garden last night?"
And while the morning sun climbed into
the Jerusalem sky, Peter denied it again,
the cock crowing while he spoke.
And at that moment Jesus turned and gazed
into Peter's eyes and Peter remembered
his own promise and Christ's words.

Thereafter, it is said Peter went out
out to the countryside and wept bitterly.
And that his sorrow was so great,
his love so strong,
he wept for three years;
that his tears were so bitter
they carved the flesh of his cheeks.
And for the rest of his days he
could not bear his own reflection
in water and shiny surfaces.
And it is said he refused to look directly

into the eyes of another for the rest of his life
and that he was unable to shed another tear,
having cried himself dry and deep.
And so that no one will ever have to suffer
the gaze of St. Peter again, we are born with
those lines in our face. The grooves that run
from the corners of our eyes to our lips.
The furrows that carry bitter tears to our tongue.

ON BEING ASKED IF THERE WAS ART OR CULTURE IN THE TOWN WHERE I GREW UP

Three times a day, at 7:00 a.m., 3:00 p.m. and 11:00 p.m., we listened to "*Fanfare for the Common Man*" when the steam whistles announced the end of the shifts.

Our Church of the Blast Furnace and the Open Hearth Cathedral enjoyed world-renowned reputations. Anonymous architects achieved a superb harmony of tall piers, columns and vaults, all realized with a sense of litheness and grace that belies the massive structure which they compose. The great North Smoke Window of the Cathedral contained an extensive and varied fenestration of smoke-stained glass, illustrating among other things, the labors of the months.

Our town's famous welders and mechanics enjoyed world-wide reputations and were inducted into the Fine Arts Burn and Scar Academy.

On Friday nights everyone was invited to the Musée des Oasis Gallery and Grille for openings of new works in the modern and contemporary styles seen in the faces of the workers, in their modern bodies, stripped of grace and delicacy.

Out for a walk in the evening we enjoyed the sweeping horizontal movement, the unadorned lines, the severe planes and over-hanging roofs, the interpenetration of inner and outer space of the Frank Lloyd Wright steel mills against the blaze-orange horizon.

The ballet of exhausted and sweaty men who moved around the slag heaps and cold draw pits of Mill 6 was bold and daring!

We had great theater, too. Who can forget the drama when our handsome, young Irish-Catholic priest ran off with the beautiful, young Italian woman who worked as a secretary at the Church Rectory Office?

And how can I forget the many evenings spent at home by the hearth reading fiction in the local newspaper: the sad tales of plant managers, told in the documentary-realism style, of forced plant closings due to worker demands and the failure of union concessions? What a great tragi-comedy that was. Our town lost 4,000 jobs in less than two years. We laughed until we cried.

Later that year, on every-other Tuesday at the Cultural Institute for the Unemployed and the Museum of Modern Welfare, we observed the Giacometti people—upright, standing figures with almost no volume rooted to the base—and the Modigliani woman—elongated, dreamy and brooding.

Back then, we longed for the union of formal beauty and spiritual content. We knew that our art and culture were not luxuries but necessities without which we would be vastly impoverished.

UNION MEETING, 1959

Once during the dark winter of 1959,
I walked with my father to a
union meeting at the AFL-CIO Hall,
where inside rumors of walkouts and strike
gathered us, and men offered
cigarettes without the asking.

When Bruno Nardelli called the meeting to order,
he said he just returned from Pittsburgh where
the owners were still unwilling to meet with him.
Then Bruno opened the floor for discussion.
Mario Tomasi said although he had twelve children,
a wife, and a mother and father living under
the same roof, he would be the first to walk
and lead his men from Plant 6 to the picket lines.
And Stavros Petrakis yelled, "Ya, me too!"
Then Marcello Rugetti stood up and shouted,
"Let the bastards carry slag to their own heaps,"
to the thundering claps of the workers.

Walking home, we passed the gates and fences
of U.S. Steel, moved toward the blast furnaces
whose burning orange lit all our lives,
the furnaces that burn year round except
for two weeks in the summer when
the whole plant shuts down,
and the lucky men get to crawl
inside to scrape them clean.
Closer, we felt flames, warm on our faces,
so we took off our coats and walked the rest
of the way home in sweatshirts and sweaters.

Beyond these fences, nothing else mattered.
The whole world was here. Later, we felt
sleet turn to snow as we made our way along
the dim streets above the frozen river,
catching glimpses of ourselves
in store windows, watching our shadows
go before us into that long night,
those fires burning deep and bright
into the center of our lives.

WORKERS

"Capital is dead labour that, vampire-like, only lives by sucking living labour, and lives the more, the more labour it sucks. "
—Karl Marx, Chapter 10, "The Working Day," **Capital**

Seven o'clock, 3 o'clock, 11 o'clock, day and night, night and day, in every steel town in the valley—Ellwood City, Beaver Falls, New Brighton, Rochester, Beaver, Monaca, Aliquippa, Ambridge, Freedom—workers *are putting on their coats, picking up their lunch buckets* filled with cold meat sandwiches, fruits, hunks of cake and pie wrapped in waxed paper, thermoses filled with steaming coffee and slipped into their snug space in the hip-roofed pails, and going off to work—*out of their houses, down through the mean streets and alleys to the mill.* Life in these towns moved to the rhythm of seven-three-eleven-seven, punctuated by steam whistles. They made their way along the cracked sidewalks, *went across the black lifeless plain of the mill yard toward the blast furnaces, looming huge in the early dusk* or dawn or night. *There were men ahead of them and behind, a straggling, silent procession.* They always arrived a little early, like good Catholics for Mass, to have their private moments. Dressed in their *shapeless, work stained clothes and heavy shoes*, they gathered across the street from the gate house, paused with friends to smoke and talk, to sit on the wooden benches outside of the bars. Others went inside for *a quick beer.* When the whistle blew the end of one shift and the beginning of another, the workers shuffled quietly toward the gate house where their time cards waited for them in the metal slots on the wall. They moved toward the gate house and merged without thought into single file, like grains of sand lining up for their descent through the neck of an hourglass. They greeted workers from the last shift with a nod or exchanged "Heys" and always with a little envy, knowing their day was done. They reached for their time cards, slipped them between the thin lips of the time clock, waited for the metal "thunk" of the clock's teeth to bite its purple time, then returned the card to its work slot on the other side of the gate house. All of this done in one sweeping motion: "thunk," "thunk," "thunk," twice a day, ten times a week, fifty times a month, 480 times a year, "thunk," "thunk," "thunk." *The voice of the mill was harsher than theirs. It came over the wall like the breathing of a giant at work, like the throb of an engine buried deep in the earth. In it were the piping of whistles and the clash of metal on metal; the chuffing of yard locomotives, the rattle of electric cranes and skip hoists, the bump-bumb-bump of a train of cars getting into motion; the wide-mouthed blow of the Bessemers; the thud of five-ton ingots dropping six inches as they were stripped of their moulds, the clean, tenpin crack of billets dropping from a magnet, the solid unhurried grind of the ore dumper, lifting a whole railroad gondola of iron ore and emptying it delicately; the high whine of the powerhouse dynamos, the brute growl of the limestone and dolomite crushers, the jolting blows of the steam hammers in the blacksmith shop, the distant, earth-shaking thunder of the booming mill's giant rolls. A hundred discords merged into harmony, the harsh, triumphant song of iron and flame.* All merged with the steady, quiet breathing of men, deep into the melody of their work. Later, when their shift was over, as they waited behind the gates with their empty lunch buckets, waited for the whistle to blow, their minds drifted to the wetness of beers; to the soothing voices of their families; to the quiet breathing of their sleeping children; to the mastery and pride of living payday-to-payday; to paid up rent, food on the table, clothes on their children's backs; to a little money jingling in their pockets; to the liberation of a day off here and there; to the week of vacation coming next summer; to all the life that was waiting for them outside this gate, on the other side of these fences. So when the whistle blew, Augustonelli, Barsontini, Carinci, DeSanzo, DeTullio, Ferrucci, Gagliardo—all of them—rushed through the gate house with certainty and precision, the "thunk" "thunk" "thunk" echoing across the yard. Some ran to their cars. Others walked toward the bars; toward their wives and children who had come to greet them and were waiting with smiles at the corner; toward the heaven of their houses waiting to take them in. And *hope sustained them all: hope and the human tendency to feel that, dreadful though one's circumstances might be at the moment, there were depths of misfortune still unplumbed beneath one, there were people much worse off . . . . And there was always hope . . . . The greater part went from day to day feeling that all this was only temporary since such things couldn't last, that just before human flesh and blood could stand no more something would happen to change everything for the better. But it never did. When human flesh and blood could stand no more it got up at six in the morning as usual and put on its work clothes and went into the mill; and when the whistle blew it came home.*

15

THE WOMAN WHO CURED FITS

I heard this one some years ago, back when I was much younger and my memory a lot better. There was this old Italian woman, the butcher's wife, who could rid people of fits and headaches and things of that sort. I remember people went to her as a last resort, in desperation, after the doctors failed.

Once a cousin of mine took one of those fits at a family reunion. It was like she was being pulled into another world, shaking and shuddering like a tree limb in wind and thunder. When she came to, she didn't remember anything. So right away my aunt and uncle take her to the butcher's wife, who asks my cousin if she wants to be free from the fits. Of course my cousin did, so the butcher's wife began speaking in a low voice, in Italian. Then she left them and walked to the back of the butcher shop, still whispering some prayer or something. She didn't return for a while, but when she did, she was carrying a long butcher's knife, sharp as a barber's razor. She then cut tiny crosses in my cousin's forehead and in the palm of each of her hands. Blood oozed from the cuts, but not too much. And all the while the woman kept whispering some Italian prayer.

Well, I guess my cousin was cured right there because she never had another fit in her life as far as I know. Must have bled the devil right out of her! At least that's what people say. Funny thing, though, is that my cousin never had scars—not on her forehead or on her palms. Not a trace of anything. Nobody ever talks about this, not even my cousin. It's like it never happened. As I remember, we never thought the butcher's wife special or anything. She was just a good neighbor. Just the woman who cured fits.

HEADACHES

Mama is at the door again, a finger raised to her lips hushing us quiet. I know that means Papa's home early from the mill, down with one of his headaches, so I tip-toe across the living room and head for my bedroom, frightened by the sight of him in his work pants and tee-shirt soaked with sweat. He has a compress made from a diaper soaked in Ben-Gay across his eyes and forehead.

Mama kneels beside him, like Mary kneeling beside Jesus after he's been taken down from the Cross. Mama listens to his moans and runs her hand through his dark, wet hair. In the quiet of my room, I beg God to let the angels of sleep carry him away the way they do me every night. On days Papa comes home with headaches we're not allowed to eat supper until he's better and can come to the table. Otherwise, Mama just tells us supper is on the stove or in the fridge and we pick and fend for ourselves.

But I love the times when his headaches go away and we eat supper later than usual. I love when Mama calls us to eat and we gather around the Formica table and sit in our chairs and Papa comes walking in looking worn out and groggy from swimming in his pain. I want to cry because he reminds me of that picture of Lazarus from the Bible, but I'm so happy I don't and just say, "Hi Papa!" And I love the way he nods and smiles and doesn't say a word, but I know he loves me, and when he sits down and Mama says our supper prayer out loud and finishes with "from thy bounty, through Christ, our Lord, Amen" I always borrow from that other prayer and whisper "Thank you for giving us this man who gives us this day our daily bread."

WHY GOD GAVE US MUSCLES

—for Gennero LaRizza

First grade. Sister Angelica is teaching us how we should raise our hands when we have to go the bathroom: a hand raised with one finger means urinate; a hand raised with two fingers means, well, you know, the other. We learn a new word for bathroom, too: *lavatory*. This should be the word we use for the rest of our school years, she tells us. When we have to go, we're supposed to raise our hand, show one or two fingers and ask if we may be excused to go to the lavatory. Survival skills for the next twelve years.

During religion lesson that morning, I notice when Gennero LaRizza raises his hand (one finger). When Sister Angelica calls on him he asks if he may be excused to go to the lavatory. But Sister snaps back "No! Why do you think God gave us muscles!" So Gennero's hand goes down and we're back to our religion. Ten minutes later I hear those hyperventilating sobs children make when they try to suppress their cries. The sounds are coming from behind me. I turn and see it's Gennero, who is now sitting in his own seat, his own pee soaking through his navy blue trousers and dripping down the chair legs to the floor. He keeps sobbing but never raises his hand again. Soon Sister Angelica hears him too and stomps back to his desk, her nostrils flaring and her cheeks turning red. Stopping at Gennero's desk, she looks down and sees the urine that surrounds his shoes, as if he stepped into a rain puddle on a sidewalk. Gennero's sobbing louder now, and the whole class is turned around looking at him.

Sister moves around behind Gennero, hovers over him for a moment, then grabs him by the shirt collar and that tuft of hair that grows on the back of the neck. Lifting him from his seat, she drags him up the aisle to the front of the room, his shoes barely scuffing along the floor. Just before Sister reaches the door, she stops and yells at us not to look up, that we should continue reading silently our religion lesson in our workbook, and that God is looking down at us and will tell her if anyone looks up. We're all staring at Sister and Gennero now, and just before I look down to my religion workbook, I notice how the skin around Gennero's neck and cheeks is being pulled tight, like a sock over a foot. Then Sister continues lifting and dragging Gennero from the room and we listen to his cries disappear down the hallway toward the boys' lavatory. We're all looking down at our religion workbooks now. It's quiet like church. God is watching us, waiting for one of us to look up. Now we know another reason why God gave us muscles.

THE DAY JOHN KENNEDY WAS SHOT

It was just after lunch. All the 7th grade boys were huddled in the dark of the school gymnasium for our monthly assembly, another film in the series entitled *Giving Your Life to God: Becoming a Priest or Brother*, grainy black and white films all 7th grade boys saw every year. In the film, a priest or brother and a young boy walk along a wooded path, heads bowed in contemplation of the young boy's future. According to the film's narrator, this represented a time just after receiving a call to the clerical life. The narrator said something about this being the most difficult decision in a young boy's life—to accept or not accept the call. "Many are called, but few are chosen," is the phrase I remember echoing through the gym as the voice of Sister Superior boomed through the p. a. system, saying that assembly period was over and that we were to return to our homeroom, where we would be joined by the girls and Sister Angelina.

Back in homeroom, sitting in silence, we were startled again by Sister Superior's voice from the p. a. explaining that just a short time ago President Kennedy was shot in Dallas and was now being operated on in a hospital near the scene of the shooting. Although we could not see Sister sitting in her little broadcasting booth attached to her office, we heard an unfamiliar quavering in her voice and knew she was on the verge of tears.

She instructed us to take out our geography and history books, kneel in the aisle next to our desk, hold one book in each hand, and extend our arms as far as we could to make them parallel with the ground. She commanded us to hold that position until further notice. If enough of us suffered, she said, perhaps God would spare the life of our Catholic President. The pain we would suffer in our seventy-two sagging 7th grade arms would be our way of taking away some of the President's pain and suffering so that he might live. She said she was signing off and that we would listen to live radio and t.v. reports from Dallas until the end of the school day, which meant about another ninety minutes. Then Walter Cronkite's scratchy, distant voice broke in: "There has been an attempt, as you might know, on the life of President Kennedy." And we fell silent.

So there we were: seventy-two sagging arms, little soldiers of Christ, little crosses kneeling in the aisles of our own Golgothas to save the President. Taking his suffering away. And we prayed. Some cried. Petey Augustino, complete with spaghetti stains on his shirt and tie, goofed around as usual. Angela Russo and Freddy Barzini giggled. Most of us dropped our arms to our sides within minutes, gravity and the weight of history and geography too much for us. Except for Donna Bennedetto who was kneeling behind me. Donna, who would be the only girl in our class to enter the convent after 8th grade, remained staunch and upright in her human cross position. How long could Donna hold out? I didn't know, but I could see intent in her eyes. How long would her frail 67 pound frame bear her up? How much suffering could she take on? In all her holiness, could Donna carry that weight? Shortly thereafter, my wondering was answered when I heard a tumbling thud and crash and turned to see Donna lying against the folding metal closet doors, her eyes rolling in the sockets under her eyelids, whispering something I didn't understand, still clutching her books, then passing out cold. Maybe this holy pact was working after all! Maybe the President would live!

After reviving Donna with smelling salts and taking her to the nurse's office, Sister Angelina returned to the room and told us we should get back in our desks, put our books away, and begin saying the rosary. For the rest of the day, Sister Angelina led us in the recitation, while Walter Cronkite continued with his reports. When the 3:30 bell shook us from our rosary trance and we were dismissed for the day, we still hadn't been told whether the President was dead or alive. Leaving the building, I saw nuns and lay teachers sobbing and embracing each other in the hallways and Nuncio, the janitor, sitting on the bottom step of the stairwell, head bowed, holding a mop in one hand and covering his eyes with the other.

Walking home, I watched the red and yellow and white lights of cars moving toward me and away from me in the fading afternoon light. At the corner of 5th and Lawrence, five steelworkers from the three o'clock shift huddled together. A thick arm held a tiny transistor radio in their midst. Nearing

Mancini's T. V. and Appliance Store, I moved to join the crowd staring through the plate glass window at the pyramid of t. v. sets. Everyone fixed upon the same sequence of black and white images repeated twenty-one times: the head of a news reporter, a car speeding down a winding street and under an overpass, then out of sight. Over and over in silence: the weeping head, the speeding car. Twenty-one times. Then twenty-one smiling faces of the young President and the little white ghost tracks of letters and numbers making their way across the bottom of the screen:

"John Fitzgerald Kennedy: 1917-1963"

The crowd moved into itself. No one spoke. No one sobbed. The great smokestacks of the city churned thick and black. Late November mist gathered and fell. Everyone listened to the silence. Everyone moved toward the dark. Everyone would reach back for that moment forever.

GRANDMOTHER'S SONG

This morning, I find myself tracing the blue and red
highway lines on a map of Pennsylvania with my finger.
I see I've drawn a circle around Torrence,
the State Hospital where my grandmother
spent a year sometime in the 1930s.
No one in the family ever talks about it.
I didn't find out about it until last summer—
fifty years after the fact. Fifty years.
Enough time for a person to live and die
and go crazy in between.

But what about Grandmother and that year?
Why was she there? No one knows for sure.
Or is willing to tell. Fatigue? Depression?
Too many children? What was the trigger?
A cousin recalls stories Grandmother told
about men and women in white and trays of food
being shoved through slots in cold metal doors.
My father, a young boy then, motherless for a year,
remembers the day they drove to Torrence
to bring her home: hot, humid,
his getting sick in the afternoon air.
Dust flying about the heads of my grandfather
and his friend who owned and drove the car.
Then the trip home in the sweltering hours.

I wonder, Grandmother, what were you thinking
that afternoon during the long drive home?
How would you return to the old life?
That first night: no locks on the doors, no strangers.
Sitting down to supper with your family,
your oldest daughter who was mother for a year,
gently setting plates of food in front of you
with so much love and delicacy,
like gifts in a sacred ritual.
I think of the stillness in the house that night
as you climbed the stairs to your room
then combed out your coal-black hair
to your waist as it never was during the day.
I think of the quiet of the room,

how it must have surrounded you
like the cloud of unknowing.
How my grandfather's touch
may have carried you back
from some dark and dusty road
you traveled that year.
I would not come to know you for twenty years,
and by then everything was forgotten,
buried in the years and miles.
The child I was never knew.

Then I came to you in the afternoons of summer,
remember the way you wiped your hands
in your apron when you saw me coming
through the grape arbor and screen door,
how you opened your arms to greet me.
And we would sit in the warm kitchen
near the window, dough rising in the oven,
me cradled in your lap, you humming
and singing songs from the radio—
not the opera of Caruso or Verdi—
but the strains of Gospel and Country Western
from WWVA, Wheeling, West Virginia.
Loss, love gone wrong, broken hearts—
that was your song.
I remember looking up into your face,
seeing your eyes staring off into the distant
afternoon, particles of flour and dust
floating and dancing in the shafts of light
spilling in from the windows that opened to the world.

Grandmother, this map shows me the way
but will never get me there. These lines tell me
nothing of that terrain, nothing of the quiet car
inching its way across the dusty miles of
Pennsylvania countryside sometime in the 1930s.
Nothing of the broken rhythms moving through your heart.

ROUTE 65

—for Rich, Johnny, Chief, Craig, Junston, Sacks, Barry, Grady

Kennedy was dead. The war raged on. One us was going to die. One of us was going to be famous. Most of us would shuffle off to that dark, anonymous city to unfamous lives that no one would remember, let alone forget. No one explained how it would happened.

But for a moment, our world was on fire, and we were burning down Route 65 along the banks of the river where the Ohio turns east toward Ohio. Saturday nights we drove broken down cars south on Route 65, singing Aretha and Stevie through those dark and smoky cities—Beaver Falls, New Brighton, Rochester, Beaver, Monaca, Aliquippa, Ambridge, Freedom. We were burning for the dance halls of New Brighton and Rochester. Burning for the dark beauty of steelworkers' daughters who stayed up late begging God to free them from the sooty shadows of the mills. And, for a moment, we were gods on Saturday night and the world was to be created. We were the scorched earth. We were the waters of the Beaver rushing into the wide Ohio. We were the barges pushing through the hard waters. We were the dirty light of morning. We were the yellow moon shoving through the smoke ash of the air, and we were the night stars boiling in the black cauldron beyond our grasp. We were the black raindrops. We were the night exploding in Jones & Laughlin orange. We were the choked weeds and the dead fruit of autumn. We were the eastern gulls diving for dead river carp. We were the open hearths. We were the molten slag dumped down river banks. We were the rolled steel and hot ingots. We were the ones who trembled in the arms of love.

We were the ones who believed the world was on fire for us, and we were burning, burning toward that city before we turned off to take our place among the lost and the nameless, to understand and keep alive with our breath the small ember of this world.

DANCING WITH SUSIE

"Bold lover, never, never canst thou kiss,
Though winning near the goal—yet do not grieve;
She cannot fade, though thou hast not thy bliss,
For ever wilt thou love, and she be fair!"
—John Keats, "Ode to a Grecian Urn"

"I'm just about at the end of my rope,
But I can't stop trying, I can't give up hope.
Because I feel that one day I'll hold you near,
Whisper I still love you. Until that day is here,
I'm crying...."
—Smokey Robinson, "Ooo Baby Baby"

Sometimes a glimpse an old photograph or a few notes from the radio of a passing car, a knock on a door, or a glance from a stranger and you're traveling down an old memory:

It's 1965 and you're slow dancing with Susie for the tenth time to "Ooo Baby Baby" by Smokey Robinson and the Miracles in the white-washed, streamer-decorated basement of her best friend. You're fifteen. It's midnight, and you're beyond curfew. But you love the smell of her perfume and the softness of her cheek against yours, the sweet taste of the thin strands of her hair in your mouth. You've never danced this close to a woman before. And there is this spinning in the center of your stomach and you want it to go on forever.

Years later, you remember Susie when the professor talks about that poem with the figures on the urn, the eternal lovers, the ones who will never kiss. And how their love is better because of this. How, frozen in this moment, they will stay forever young and burn in their forever passion, poised at the edge of their bliss. That a song not sung is sweeter than one heard is an argument you've never believed or found comforting, not for a moment. Not then.

And not now. When you find yourself talking about this poem with your students, you do so without the conviction that the thinking was sweeter than the doing. But that dancing with Susie was so much better than the thought of dancing with Susie. That the dancing done is always better than the dancing not done.

So when the knock comes, or the glance from across the room, and it all returns—the smell of perfume in the midnight air, the softness of the cheek forever warm and young, the sweet taste of hair brushing your lip—-you smile. And the world spins inside of you forever.

REMEMBERING BULL DeLISIO

Twenty years later, you cannot forget him,
you cannot escape his gaze from another world.
The blurred smile in black and white.
He will be here in your high school
yearbook forever, the memorial page.
These thin black lines measuring
the brevity of his life.
Not enough life to have known life.

You remember:
dusk, old Italians living
near the river's edge
walking in their gardens;
the shiny green smell of tomatoes;
the slap of wooden screen doors
echoing along the river;
the flickering of moths
against bare yellow porch lights;
the boys going down to the river.

Then it happens:
The sudden swirl of the river,
a moment's bubble burst of brightness
before the brilliant dark.
Boys, cold and wet, out of breath,
come running up the hill, crying
"He didn't come up! He didn't come up!"

You remember the rescue team
dragging the river, tossing grapple lines;
the thud of aluminum boats against rock;
the skittering path of searchlights
cutting the falling dark. Then always
the hook winning out over flesh,
the river giving up its kill when ready.

Bull, every summer in a dream
I go down with you, the descent
to the watery nowhere.
Whatever worlds came to you then,
whatever words were lost in the ripples,
whatever life gathered in the swirl,
I carry back to strangers, friends, loved ones,
yesterday, tomorrow, now, now.
And always I rise in the waking.

PAUSING UNDER A STREETLIGHT

Some evening you might be wandering
the streets of your home town, and suddenly,
pausing under a streetlight to strike a match,
you would be struck by the weight of it—
all those years gone by.
How would you change things?
What would you ask for?
Another name? Another face?
Maybe you'd be the one others
would follow, dress like?
All the failed followers flocking to you
when you walked into the drugstore.
Maybe you'd be the one to come back
from California during the summer of '67
with long hair and mystical zodiac patterns
stitched in your jeans by a blonde flower-child.
Maybe your dream would grow and widen?
A hero? Maybe.

But maybe it's the way life gathers
in this moment, the way it all comes back
in the swirl of memory, in a beam of light:
compassion, forgiveness, understanding.
Turning up your collar, maybe you'd step back
into the night, this small light shining your way toward home.
No regret, no sadness, no blame.

STORY PROBLEMS

—for Mario Morini, 5th grade math teacher

A farmer buys 60 bushels of potatoes for $104.00. For one kind
he pays $1.80 per bushel, and for another kind he pays $1.60 per
bushel. How many bushels of each kind of potato did he buy?
Four hours after a boy starts from a certain point on a bicycle at
the rate of 12 mph, he is followed by a man with an automobile
and is overtaken in 8 hours. How fast is the man in the car
going? How far may a man walk into the country at the rate of 4
mph if he rides back at the rate of 20 mph and must be home in 8
hours? I have twice as many dimes as nickels and 10 more
quarters than the number of dimes and nickels combined. If I
have $8.50 in all, how many coins do I have, and how many
bushels of potatoes can I buy from the farmer in the first story?
Mary is 24 years old. Mary is twice as old as Ann was when
Mary was as old as Ann is now. How old is Ann and is she old
enough to drive and date? Two trains leave different stations at
the same time and travel in opposite directions, one going twice
as fast as the other. At the end of 4 hours, they are 216 miles
apart. How much do the dry martinis cost in the dining car?
Mrs. Jones buys a chicken weighing 3 3/4 lbs. How much will it
cost her at 61¢ per lb., and what should she serve with it for
dinner? Art and Bill have 80 marbles between them. Art wins
from Bill as many marbles as Art originally had, and then he has
3 times as many as Bill. How old is Bill's sister from New
Jersey? A truck leaves an interchange in upstate New York and
travels east at an average rate of 50 mph. A passenger car
traveling east at the same rate of speed leaves the interchange 24
minutes later with 7 passengers aboard at an average age of 47
years. If the passenger car maintains an average speed of 58
mph, what make and year will the car be by the time the truck
reaches Akron, Ohio? A farmer starts to town in his '57 Chevy
pickup truck hauling 100 125-lb. bales of hay. Along the way he
hits another pickup truck carrying 600 chickens weighing 3 3/4
lbs. each. How old is the farmer's wife?

James buys 18 gallons of gas at 89¢ per gallon. How much
change would he receive from a $10.00 bill if he bought the same
amount of gas in 1967 when gas cost 29¢ per gallon when he
drove his mother to the hospital which was 32 miles away in

31

upstate New York after she broke her leg, which healed at the rate of 250 millimeters per day in a 10 mph wind gusting at times to 25-20 mph with small craft warnings on area lakes and the possibility of thunderstorms later tonight giving way to clear and sunny skies tomorrow? If a girl walks at the rate of 2 mph to the home of her friend who lives 24 miles away in a Cape Cod style home with 3 bedrooms up, 1 1/2 baths down and French Provincial furniture which her parents purchased from Cal's House of Furniture Going-Out-of-Business Sale last week at a 40% discount, how long will it take her to find her way there if she stops to make a recipe for spice cake which serves 6 people and calls for 1 3/4 cups of sugar per person if the sugar costs 15¢ per pound in 1957, but this is 1988 and the rate of inflation has pushed the cost of sugar as high as the number of marbles Art won from Bill in 1966, which was the year of Art's 16th birthday which made him twice as old as Mary was when she was half as old as Ann is now but younger than the farmer's wife who is delivering 600 3 3/4-lb. chickens from upstate New York to Dayton--no--Akron, Ohio, in a pickup truck going 67 mph and following a train going twice as fast on tracks that are twice as expensive per foot as the cost of sugar in 1957, factoring in the rate of inflation and cost of living expenses for that year for a family of 4 living on a fixed income of $8,000 per year?

Let $\underline{x} = \underline{y}$ in all of the above equations and let $\underline{a} = \underline{\text{your decision}}$ to become an English major when you decide to go to college in 1969, when the rate of inflation is equal to your heart rate monitored at the time you turned the page of your SAT Examination Booklet and read DO NOT TURN THE PAGE UNTIL YOU ARE INSTRUCTED TO DO SO! And while working on those story problems in 1969 you made a quick, sharp 180° turn at 67 mph in a strong head wind and ever since your life has never been quite the same.

II
INTERMEZZO

DEDICATED TO THOSE OF
ST. AGATHA PARISH
WHO SERVED IN THE WARS
OF OUR COUNTRY

WHEN THE ITALIANS CAME TO MY HOME TOWN

E l'America l'è lunga e l'è larga;
L'è circondata da monti e colline.
E con l'industria dei nostri italiani,
Abbiam formato paesi e città.

And America is long and vast;
It is surrounded by mountains and hills.
And by the hard work of our Italians,
We built towns and cities

—Italian Folksong

When the Italians came to my home town in the 1880s, they were not welcomed by those settlers who had preceded them. The "dusky foreigners," as they were referred to in a newspaper account of the time, were sold the land across the county line where there would be no roads, electricity or sewers for another thirty years. In a 1942 history of my home town, Henry W. Hartman, the city father, was compared to George Washington because Hartman did for my home town what Washington did for our country—both were described as men who always had the people's "welfare at heart." The "Father" of my home town, whose name would come to grace one of my home town's public elementary schools, sold the Italians that land. By 1923, the children of those dusky foreigners Mr. Hartman brought to his fledgling city to build his railroads were being educated in the classrooms of the Hartman School and continue to be educated there to this day.

Between 1880 and 1920, over 4 million Italian immigrants entered the United States, a little more than half of those arriving between 1901 and 1910. Of the more than 8 million European immigrants coming to the U. S. during that decade, one in four came from Italy. Of those two million Italian arrivals between 1901-1910, about 67,000 settled in Pennsylvania, and between 1910-20 nearly 200,000 more found their way to Penn's Woods.

Of that number, I am uncertain how many came to western Pennsylvania to join the labor crews (or "Wop Gangs" as they were sometimes called) which built roads and railroads or to forge their fortunes in the steel mills; what I do know, however, is that the flow of immigrants to this area was such that it created a density of Italian immigrants surpassed only by the Italian colonies in the metropolitan areas of New York, New Jersey and Chicago. By 1900, the population of my home town was recorded as 2,243. By 1920 it had nearly quadrupled to 8,958, with approximately 30% of the population of Italian descent.

Henry Waters Hartman came of age during an era when great fortunes were made by the barons of industry whom we read about in the old history books. By the 1890s, Mr. Hartman had successfully established himself in the manufacturing of steel wire, wire nails, wire mats, woven fences and cold rolled steel, and secured a reputation sufficient enough to allow him to join hands with Andrew Carnegie. Hartman would later dispose of his interests in the partnership with Carnegie who shortly afterwards, created his powerful Carnegie Steel Company, the predecessor of United States Steel Corporation.

The first Italians began arriving in the area in 1885, and in 1892 my home town was incorporated. The first person born in my home town after incorporation was Maria Fresca, the daughter of Italian immigrants. *Fresca* roughly translated means "fresh" or "recent," an appropriate name for the newborn child of newly arrived immigrant parents to this new world settling in this newly incorporated city. By the time I got to know the descendants of the Fresca family, they were known by the flat, unlyrical, anglicized version of the name, Frisk.

Hartman's plans to turn my home town into a manufacturing city necessitated the flow of goods in and out of the area by train. To get trains in and out of the area necessitated the building of railroads. And the building of railroads necessitated a labor force. Hartman's railroads were mostly constructed by Italian immigrant labor. Hartman hired Luigi Parillo as the padrone and entrusted him with the duties of transporting Italian immigrants to America. Among the men Parillo brought to this country to put down Hartman's rails were Gennaro Frisk (Fresca), Tony Flori, Joe Moliterno, Tony Gotti, Pasquale Rocco, and Gennero Mazzei. Among the many pre-industrial skills these men brought to the new world were stone cutting and masonry, fortunate for an area rich with sandstone and limestone quarries. Much of the limestone from Duck Run Quarry, one of the largest quarries in the area, was taken by Italian stonemasons—among them, Louie Parillo, Joe Condi, Joe Reino, Ralph Suglia, John Paglia, Frank Albino—who carried their native trades with them across the Atlantic, as would my Grandfather DeTullio some twenty years later. Some of these men had learned their trades in the quarry regions of Tuscany, some near Massa and Carrara, where nearly four hundred years earlier marble blocks had been cut, lifted and delivered to a young stonemason in Florence named Michaelangelo Buonarroti.

The litany of these railsplitter and stonemasons' names rings familiar to me today because sixty years later, their grandchildren carried them into the classrooms of the Catholic school we attended. When the nuns called morning rolls, the names were not unlike those called from steerage lists at Ellis Island, the ones kept by Hartman's *padrones*, or the quarry bosses.

By the turn of the century, however, most of these men had given up full time stone masoning for the steel mills which, by the early 1900s, were booming throughout the west-central valley of western Pennsylvania. Stone for steel. But even though their steady work and livelihoods now came from steel, the men continued to practice their stone cutting when they could, often hiring themselves out in the evenings or on weekends to build handcut limestone and sandstone retaining walls for the many new homes being built on the hillsides in the area, a result of the new prosperity. And they were always quick to lend their skills to the Church whenever stone or brick repairs were needed. When many of the men lost their jobs in the mills during the Depression, the WPA organized and hired the Italian stone cutters—at a fraction of their mill wages—to build schools and any number of other limestone structures which still stand today, long after the mills have been torn down and sold for scrap metal.

As a six year old in 1957, I studied the stone cutting movements of the Greco brothers, both recent arrivals from Italy, whom my father hired to build a retaining wall for the driveway of our new house. I was dazzled by the speed and accuracy with which they could twirl a 10 lb. slab of sandstone in the palm of their left hands and tap away the unnecessary stone with the hammer held tightly in their right hands, allowing the stone to fit snugly in the wall where it remains to this day. I sat mesmerized on the stone steps and watched these olive-skinned men in their wide-brimmed hats and white shirts buttoned to the collar (buttoning my top shirt button is a habit I practice to this day—did I pick up this fashion tip from the Greco brothers?), practicing their sleight-of-hand while talking to each other in rapid-fire Italian which sounded like a 45 r.p.m. record cranked to 78 r.p.ms!

Not long ago, I found an old photograph of my Grandfather DeTullio standing among a dozen or so of the local Italian stone cutters in front of an elementary school they were hired to build by the WPA. I recognize many of the men as my Grandfather's neighbors and family friends, as well as the grandfathers of many of my childhood friends. The men are staring directly into the eye of the camera, looking tough, with not a smile among them. My Grandfather, arms akimbo, stands solid and firm as the limestone blocks he quarried. He is dressed in the same gray canvas work clothes I remember him wearing all the time, and the look on his face and in his eyes is the one I recognize in his formal wedding photograph with my Grandmother Josephine Mancinelli DeTullio that I have hanging in my study.

Today, in front of St. Agatha Church—one of the two Catholic churches in my home town—stands a limestone grotto, built by my Grandfather Joe DeTullio, my mother's father, in honor of the Virgin Mary and dedicated to those who served in the wars of our country. I pass the church and the grotto a dozen times or more during my once-or-twice-a-year visits home, since my parents now live three blocks from the church. In the evening, the white marble Virgin Mary inside the dark stone grotto is bathed by a floodlight. If you watch the passing cars closely, you can even see the good Catholics making the sign of the cross, and they're probably whispering a little prayer to her, too. But when I pass by, I see my Grandfather in his gray canvas work clothes and wide-brimmed hat working the stone, limestone chips flying from the quick strikes of his hammer against a chisel grasped tightly by a callused and dusty left hand. I imagine his hands holding and caressing the limestone chunks, the way a father might cradle his new born baby. I see him setting the newly formed blocks into place for leveling and forming the grotto's base and eventual arch. My mother tells me the grotto was his gift to the Church, and I don't doubt for a moment that it was. But in some ways, I also know it was his gesture of holding onto a part of him which he knew he was losing. It is his *David*, his *Pietà*.

By 1890, when the Italians were quarrying limestone, grading roads and putting down rails, local newspapers reported rumors that Italians living in the settlements (where Mr. Hartman had sold them the land) "were reduced to the extremity of eating cats and dogs." The newspaper story also discounted the rumor, reporting that they were poor but were doing fairly well, an average worker in a steel mill earning about $1.45 a day. Approximately 200 Italians employed by the Pennsylvania Company Railroad and the Pennsylvania & Lake Erie rail were reported to be "living like sheep in a pen. A band of 20 or more have headquarters in the second story of a large brick room." It was suggested that this was the way Italians saved money—by going without luxuries. Consciously or unconsciously, newspapers were shaping public feeling and attitudes toward these dusky foreigners in their accounts of immigrant living conditions. Here is how H. M. Phelps, in a 1905 issue of the *Pittsburgh Survey*, described a typical urban Italian street scene: "Throngs of greasy, unkempt Italians standing around in front of crazy little grocery stores, jabbering and smoking while white slovenly women with filthy youngsters sit on steps or parade up and down in the streets strewn with vegetables, filthy water and rubbish of all kinds."

The irony, of course, is that many of the people against whom these charges were being leveled were unable to read English. Often poorly educated and illiterate, many of the new immigrants were unable to read newspapers in their native language, let alone the language of their newly adopted homeland. The true audience for these remarks, I suspect, was the English-speaking and reading audience, with the intent to draw a caricature so hideous and despicable as to justify mistreatment. I do not detect a desire to understand in Phelps' remarks. The accused are left to stand mute against their accusers.

The rails were also efficient at delivering cheap Italian labor. Within a day or two of a request for immigrant labor, local contractors could order carloads of recently landed immigrants from New York to job sites in western Pennsylvania. When Hartman's Pittsburgh Company needed cheap water and electric current, a dam was constructed to harness the waters of the Connoquenessing Creek. When the excavation began in the fall of 1900, an employee of the Company traveled to the emigration office in Pittsburgh and declared his needs. The emigration officer in charge called to the group of men standing around: "Any of you that want to go where this man wants you to, just step to one side." Sixteen Italian men were picked from those who stepped aside and returned to build the dam as well as kill the hundreds of copperhead snakes that inhabited the site.

The 1942 history of my home town records that these sixteen men remained with the company for years and "became excellent citizens." For a foreigner to become a model citizen, all he had to do was quit standing around, step forward, and "go where the man wants you to go." One of the workers, Mr. Seriani, a shoe maker and cobbler by trade, was told that because he was "faithful in his work" for over a year, he would be "released" from his work and helped to start a shoe shop. Servitude echoes in the language. The recorded history also reports "that a great debt of gratitude is due these pioneer Italians, 'whose hard work and sacrifices amid numerous obstacles made possible the founding" of my home town; but the history does not record what those obstacles were. Among them must surely be counted racism, servitude, prejudice and racial hostility toward these unkempt dusky throngs of greasy men and slovenly women.

40

The first Catholics to arrive in my home town were of Irish and English descent, as can be witnessed from the roster of first pastors at the Irish-Catholic church: Fathers Dwyer, O'Neill, Dooley, O'Connell, Maloney, Murphy and Wilkey. But in 1885, a wood-framed church was erected, dedicated to and named in honor of Saint Agatha, the Sicilian virgin who rejected the sexual advances of a Roman senator. Hagiography has it that the love-spurned senator ordered Agatha's breasts cut off. Through the intercession of St. Peter, however, who appeared in her jail cell and applied a celestial ointment, her breasts were restored. As if that was not enough, St. Agatha was then confined to a house of shame, along with Aphrodesia and her six shameless daughters. When authorities tried to burn Agatha at the stake, a nearby volcano erupted and her life was once again spared. The authorities finally succeeded in martyring St. Agatha. This time, foregoing the less dramatic and public for the tried and proven—they cut off her head.

Understandably, her name is invoked against breast disease, fires and volcanic eruptions. And understandably, she's also the patron saint of wet nurses. But not understandably she is the patron saint of bell ringers. Let me explain.

As I child I remember images of St. Agatha from a painting that hung in the great limestone Gothic Church, which replaced the wood-framed structure in 1918, as well as from the stamped images of her on the little sterling silver medals my Irish-Italian cousins (whose families attended St. Agatha Church) wore around their necks. St. Agatha is traditionally depicted as carrying her severed mammaries on a platter. Evidently, sometime during the Middle Ages a monk mistook them for bells or for loaves of bread. Thus the bell-ringer connection. (You might also think that she would be the patron saint of bakers, but that honor is given to Elizabeth of Hungary. Against the law of the authorities, Elizabeth concealed bread in her clothing when she visited the poor. When the authorities heard rumor that she was carrying contraband, they stopped her and ordered her to open her robes, whereupon thousands of rose petals spilled forth. A more appropriate image for a Saint!) Over time, the mammaries on St. Agatha's platter turned into bells and tiny loaves of bread. On her Feast Day—February 5—the priests at St. Agatha parish continue to bless loaves of bread.

By 1916 the pews of St. Agatha were overflowing with Italian-Catholic immigrant families, most of whom did not understand the holy rites of the Mass offered in English. This proved to be an enormous strain on the ministry of the Anglo-Irish priests of St. Agatha. Most disturbing (and today somewhat comical) however, was the ministering of the sacraments—especially the sacrament of Confession. The Irish Confessores—who neither spoke nor understood Italian--were hearing the Confessions of these new immigrants being whispered to them in the confines of the confessional booths! The idea of Irish priests absolving sinful Italians was too much for Father Wilkey, who wisely—and in desperation—petitioned the Diocese of Pittsburgh for a priest fluent in Italian to minister to the growing Italian colony of over 200 families. Bishop Canevin responded, and within a year, Father Salvatore Marino (who was born, raised, educated and ordained in Palermo, where he had served as secretary to Cardinal Lualdi) arrived in my home town and rescued the Irish Confessores from the linguistic torture and horror of their confessionals.

On July 4, 1916, ground was broken for a new Catholic church whose mission was to minister to the growing Italian colony. The dedicatory sermons were delivered by Father O'Shea in English and Father Marino in Italian. In March of 1917, the first Church of the Purification of the Blessed Virgin Mary (always and affectionately shortened to BVM) was dedicated by Archbishop Canevin of Pittsburgh, and Father Marino, a man who described as knowing the hearts and dreams of the Italian immigrants, was installed as its first Pastor. Only one sermon was delivered—in Italian—by Father DeMita, a parish pastor from a nearby town.

In 1929, Father Galliano arrived from Paterson, New Jersey, to replace Father Marino. The Diocese made a wise move transferring Father Galliano from Paterson—where the first factory in America was built—to my home town, which itself was quickly becoming an industrial center for steel makers and fabricators. Placing in the pulpit an Italian-born pastor with experience of ministering to blue-collar workers and their families was a stroke of Diocesan genius and common sense.

Like his predecessor, Father Galliano was Italian-born. Educated by the Christian Brothers, he held a Doctor of Divinity degree from the Teologico Juridico of Benevento, Italy, his birthplace, and for a time served as Monsignor of Benevento Cathedral. When Father Galliano arrived in my home town, he must have felt welcome as well as pleasantly surprised to discover an immigrant family bearing the same name as the river which flowed through his childhood home—the *Tammaro*. Thirty years later, when I was a student at the Catholic school of my parish, long after Father Galliano had been reassigned, his name was spoken in reverential whispers and tones usually reserved for saints and the Holy Virgin.

Within a year of his arrival, Father Galliano decided that the first church was too small for the growing parish, so he arranged for the purchase of a square of land next to a nearby factory. Along with the land came the old Methodist Episcopal church building, which was completely remodeled and became the new BVM Church. When it was dedicated in March, 1930, sermons were once again preached—this time in English by Bishop Boyle, and in Italian by a guest pastor, Father DeVivo.

During the 1920s and 1930s, the BVM parish continued to grow and prosper, despite the economic hardships brought on by the Great Depression, suggesting just how important and significant a role the Church played in the lives and hearts of its families. By 1940, Father Galliano and other church leaders decided it was necessary to remodel the present church to accommodate the parish's burgeoning membership.

It was also under Fr. Galliano's leadership that the parish welcomed the arrival of the Sisters of the Order of Saint Francis. In addition to providing religious instruction, especially to the children of the parish members (the parish's Catholic school would not open until 1945), the Sisters devoted their time to the social and missionary work of the parish as well as offering private instructions for violin, piano, sewing and embroidery. The Sisters were also responsible for establishing the Boy's Choir, the same one I would audition for in the autumn of 1961.

Not blessed with a musical ear or vocal chords, I was unsuccessful in my audition, and eventually found my way to the ranks of the altar boys. I quickly became adept at Latin—at least the Latin of the Mass—and served accordingly for the next five years. During my childhood, I wrestled with the notion that somehow being an altar boy was second-rate, that we were really failed choir boys, and the nuns were showing us pity by offering us the opportunity to join the altar boys.

But this inferiority complex was put to rest when I read the story of St. John Berchmans, the Belgian Jesuit boy-saint and patron of altar boys and teenagers. His virtue was such that by the time he was nine he was serving mass twice a day, seven days a week, claiming that if he didn't become a saint when he was twenty-five, he would never become one. As you might have guessed, John Berchmans, then a novice Jesuit in Rome, died from a summer fever at the age of twenty-two; his childhood wish had come true. For me, the matter was settled: an altar boy came to his calling because of his virtue, a choir boy because of his voice. A least in my mind, voice could never hold a candle to virtue.

It was also Fr. Galliano's vision that resulted in the building of the first parish parochial school. When the doors of the Purification of the Blessed Virgin Mary School opened in 1945, the nuns of the Order of the Sisters of the Religious Teachers Fillipini were there to greet the children, and they continue to do so today. The Order took its name from St. Lucy Fillipini, who founded the order of Italian teaching nuns in 1692. (St. Lucy Fillipini is not to be confused with the other St. Lucy, the Patron Saint of Gondoliers and Lamplighters, who is always pictured with her eyeballs in the palm of her hand). Known to her followers as the Spiritual Mother of Saintly Teachers, Lucy evidently showed teacherly inclinations as a child in her Etruscan village of Tarquinia, thirty-five miles northwest of Rome. By the age of seven, Lucy—whose baptismal name Lucia means "light"—was orphaned; by eight, she was building little altars around her house; and by ten she was explaining the Catechism to her peers.

Lucy opened her first school in 1707 in Rome, along the Via delle Chiavi d' oro—the street of the Golden Keys. But it would be more than two hundred years before St. Lucy's teacher-nuns would first arrive in the United States, in 1910 in Trenton, New Jersey, to work with the flood of Italian immigrants and their children who had been arriving by the thousands during that first decade of the new century. Eventually, Lucy's nuns fanned out across the country to teach by virtue and example of St. Lucy and in accordance to the rule of the Order. I recall the stories we were told about St. Lucy's heroic virtue and miracles which led to her Beatification and eventual sainthood in 1930.

Perhaps the most remarkable story of St. Lucy's life that remains with me is the one about the opening of her coffin in 1858, 126 years after her death from cancer and her burial under the floor of Our Lady's Chapel in the Cathedral Church in Montefiascone, the site of the Motherhouse of the Order. Why someone decided to open her burial vault is beyond me—perhaps it is what people did when they sensed that they might have a potential saint on hand.

In 1858, in the presence of the Superior of the Order, the Bishop, and other church officials and village witnesses, the coffin was raised from its vault and the body exhumed. To the astonishment of all those present, the hyacinths which were placed at Lucy's feet at her funeral in 1732 were still fresh, their grape and honey fragrance spilling from her coffin and filling the musty Cathedral air. As if that were not enough, Lucy's body was nearly uncorrupted, with only her burial garments showing signs of decomposing.

Another image of St. Lucy that remains with me is from a picture I once saw in her biography: one of those simple line drawings that illustrates a miraculous moment in the life of a saint. As so often happens in such attempts to literalize these occasions, the drawing seems a caricature of the event, trivializing and rendering to the point of silliness the moment it hopes to portray as inspirational. Evidently, during a Mass that Lucy was attending, at the point where the priest consecrates and breaks the Host, a fragment of the wafer fell from the priest's hands.

Instead of falling into the chalice or onto the floor, the fragment somehow (miraculously?) found its way to Lucy, who was kneeling some distance from the altar where the priest was saying Mass and was deposited on her tongue. In the drawing, the Host fragment has little wings and is flying through the church like a tiny butterfly toward Lucy whose mouth is on the verge of opening in surprise.

Humility, chastity, poverty, devotion, obedience (what better virtues to instill in little parochial school children, especially obedience!), Lucy possessed them all. She was one of those child saints whose behavior the nuns were constantly encouraging us to emulate. She was also known to have healed the sick, saved the arm of a woman from the physician's bone saw, and calmed storms. But Lucy also liked to fast a great deal, and when she did eat it was not uncommon for her to nibble stale bread crusted with mildew. Lucy practiced extreme austerity and personal mortification. There are stories of young girls flocking to Lucy, begging her to slap them in the face and to forgive them. Other children begged Lucy's pardon for their sins and traced crosses on the ground with their tongues (the practice of tongue dragging was not uncommon among southern Italian peasants). Some children even asked Lucy to step on them, so that they could then thank her and kiss her feet. I've often wondered if this penchant for punishment and mortification was a source for much of the frequent, unquestioned corporal punishment used in our school during the 1950s.

On the day of her Beatification in 1926, St. Lucy was said to have cured the tuberculosis in one of her Order's nuns and, a few days later, the bronchopneumonia of a young boy. Having died herself of chest and lung cancer, St. Lucy is often prayed to by those afflicted with those diseases.

I remember as a child placing hyacinths at the base of the painting of St. Lucy Fillipini which hung in our school on her May 11 Feast Day. As someone who spent ten years training to be a teacher and the last sixteen years teaching, I've often wondered how much of St. Lucy's influence was responsible for my choice of vocation.

Should you ever find yourself walking the main aisle of the Sistine Chapel in Rome, look for the statue of St. Lucy Fillipini. You might even catch the grape and honeyed scent of hyacinths.

The Purification of the Blessed Virgin Mary School graduated its first class in 1951, the year of my birth. Less than five years later, in the fall of 1956, I found myself standing at those doors--not very eager to walk through them, according to my mother, who says I screamed, kicked and cried bloody murder--to begin my nine years of parochial schooling. Looking back, I imagine those screams as premonitions of the years to come—some of the most troubled and traumatic periods of my life.

When the cornerstone of the new addition of that great brick and limestone church of my Catholic youth was blessed on that Sunday in April, 1940, the dedicatory sermons were still preached in English and Italian. What made it all the more wonderful was that stepping from the main church doors onto the steps of the Italian colony's newly remodeled ediface that afternoon, the proud Italian parishioners only had to look across the street to see Henry Hartman's public school. The namesake of the man who sold some of their fathers and mothers the undeveloped land outside the city's limits to keep them away from the rest of the townsfolk now shared the same city block with the dusky foreigners' house of worship. Had Henry Waters Hartman been alive and walking the neighborhood that April afternoon, he would have heard the beautiful soprano voice of Amelia Cerriani—along with the accompanying organ music which was electronically amplified from inside the church—swirling and winding its way through the heavenly afternoon air.

This newly remodeled building would be the Catholic Church of my boyhood—the church where I would be baptized eleven years later, make my first confession (I would always add an extra number to my tally of sins just in case I gave the wrong number), take my First Communion, and stand for Confirmation when I became a Soldier of Christ. It would be the church where I would serve hundreds of daily and Sunday masses, including wedding and funeral masses.

With stained-glassed windows, plaster statues of saints with horrific, bloody gashes in their thighs and plucked eyeballs in the palms of their hands, the snow-white Carrara marble altar rail and floors—this was the church of my youth, where, as an altar boy during Holy Week, I carried three-foot tapers in their golden sticks, thick and long as baseball bats, during the Stations of the Cross; this was the church where I stood and knelt in awe when the Benedictines came to chant the Litany of the Saints in Latin during Forty Hours Devotion. And this was the church that I watched razed with a wrecking ball one afternoon in 1969 after it was desanctified and stripped of its windows, its statuary, its Carrara marble and its great wooden pews, the seats of which had been worn smooth as any fine Italian silk. The mission that was established in 1917 with the specific charge to minister to the Italian colony of 200 families and 1,000 parishioners had, by 1969, swelled to over 1200 families and nearly 5,000 parishioners.

The Church fathers had decided that the 1940 structure was too small and too costly to repair or remodel again, so they voted to build a new, more modern church, whose interior and exterior design and architecture would reflect and incorporate the progressive spirit of Vatican II. Of the new building's interior design, the local newspaper reported that there were to be none of the "trappings" of an earlier age—stained glass windows, a preponderance of statues, and ornate embellishments of the altar. The emphasis, the article reported, was to be on the physical comforts that the old church did not provide—air conditioning, a vast loud speaker system, restrooms in the vestibule and electrical snow and ice removal around the church walks. The Catholic Church had survived scandals, Crusades, Inquisitions, Schisms, Reformations and Counter-Reformations for nearly two thousand years. Suddenly, we had to free ourselves of the trappings of an older age and make way for air conditioning, loudspeakers, bathrooms and heated sidewalks—the trappings of the modern age. I wondered then, as I do now, who was really being trapped.

Without its 50 foot bell-tower with Angelus bells, this new building might be mistaken for any number of undistinguished-looking government office buildings where bureaucrats go to do their bureaucratic things. This square, tired-looking gray concrete building was constructed in the postmodern style, you might say, though no one used the term back then. Gone were the steps rising to meet the doors, where you were literally above ground-level, feeling as if you had left this earthly plane and ascended to a realm somewhere between earth and heaven. Gone were the stained glass windows.

Gone was the Carrara marble, and marble altar rail. Gone was the plaster and marble statuary. Gone were the tiered altar space and the ornately carved white wooden altar, which always looked as though it was floating above the floor. Replacing it was a five-ton block of smooth black granite. The altar hunkered solid and firm on the same level as the worshipers.

When parishioners came to celebrate the first Mass in the new building at sunrise on Easter morning of 1970, they found the old familiarity and warmth of their sacred space replaced by this spare and austere cavern, looking more like a civic auditorium or university lecture hall than a church. Many parishioners who had grown up and taken their sacraments in the old church found it difficult to warm up to and embrace the new one. The following Sunday, some of the old timers were found taking their Masses in the gothic limestone church of St. Agatha.

In the arc of history between 1885, when the Italians came to my home town, and 1969, when the new, Post Vatican II parish church was sanctified, something more than a building had been lost and replaced. When the sermons were delivered on the afternoon of the new church's dedication, they were preached in English only, though the presence of the original Italian colony continued to be evident in the presence of those who presided: Father DeBlasio, the current pastor; Father Biondi, a former pastor; Monsignor Fabbri; and the vicar and general chancellor from the Diocese of Pittsburgh, Monsignor Anthony Bosco. The mix and tumble of Italian and English vowels and consonants—which bounced their way through my home town and my youth, causing parishes to be split and churches to be built, was gone. Gone, too, was the Latin Mass which I learned as a young boy and allowed me to serve as an altar boy for many years, and which also served as a kind of linguistic thread that stitched me to my childhood classmates and friends who spoke Italian because their families permitted Italian to be spoken in their households—unlike my parents, whose own parents prohibited them from speaking the language of the old country while growing up, for fear that they would be identified as the son or daughter of a dusky foreigner and kept from their American dream.

By 1980, the postmodern structure began showing premature signs of deterioration, including the roof, which began to leak shortly after its completion. Thin-walled construction cried out for soundproofing, and an inefficient, costly and poorly designed recessed lighting system begged to be replaced. In less than ten years, the free standing Angelus bell tower began cracking. It seems that its postmodern architect forgot to cap the tower walls with a deflecting material, allowing water to run down the sides of the concrete structure. Consequently, tower sections had to be cut and replaced. Had the tower's designer consulted any number of the parish's resident stone masons, he would have been warned of this potentially dangerous flaw.

The sparse, minimalist church interior and altar space began to reshape itself, too. Postmodern screens, originally suspended above the altar—perhaps suggestive of the icon screens of the old Byzantine altars—were eventually replaced by a larger-than-life crucifix which, too, was suspended precariously above the altar. The figure of the Giacometti-like Christ, draped with loin cloth, hinted of the statuary adorning the older churches.

Even Pastor Dascenzo's mother got caught up in the remodeling (I think of it more as restoration) of the new church by donating oak trees from her back yard, which were hewn into beautiful planks, shaped into panels and placed behind the altar. With the crucifix, the panels drew and focused the parishoner's eye toward the altar's center, unlike before when the eye was left to roam the cavernous interior space. The lobby was remodeled and new doors were designed and set in place. The modernist Madonna and Child metal design on the door's glass suggested stained-glass patterns. Parisioners remarked that a wonderful looking church was made even more spectacular, though I suspect they meant that the building was finally looking more than ever like a church.

Not long ago, my mother sent me a clipping from my home town newspaper reporting the discovery of the original stained glass windows from the remodeled 1940 church in the basement of a nearby church. Plans were being made to restore as many of the windows as possible and to display them as decorative panels rather than functional windows in the new church. A piece of Carrara marble was also found, and plans for its restortion and display were being discussed.

Last year, during a Christmas visit home, I attended Mass on Christmas day. I wasn't surprised to find that a few statues had found their way into the church, and that modern Stations-of-the-Cross panels graced the north, east and west walls. Near the baptismal font and lobby, I spotted the stained glass windows, framed in wrought iron, and suspended from the ceiling, catching the late morning light, spreading Chartres-blue hues around the baptistry. And a snow-white section of carved marble, also framed and suspended with the windows—relics from another era—carried me to another time and another church. Perhaps something was returning; perhaps something had never left.

III

"You will see, my dearest father, that I wish nothing to be concealed from you, for I am careful to describe to you not only my life in general but even my individual reflections. And I beseech you, in turn, to pray that these vague wandering thoughts of mine may some time become firmly fixed, and, after having been vainly tossed about from one interest to another, may direct themselves at last toward the single, true, certain, and everlasting good."

—Francis Petrarch, "Letter to Dionisio da Borgo San Sepolcro"

LOOKING FOR MY FATHER AT REMAGEN BRIDGE

For thirty years I have looked for you coming across the smoky ruins of the Remagen bridge. In old newsreels, always hoping to spot you hopping across the charred ties, I hunkered down near the TV, sure you are among the gray ghost soldiers moving across the screen. I've even sat through *The Bridge at Remagen* a half-dozen times, imagined you were Ben Gazzara or Robert Vaughn.

On the 40th anniversary of the Allied capture of the Remagen bridge, I almost sent you a clipping from the newspaper, an interview with a local vet who reminisced about the joys of taking the bridge, the pleasure of seeing bloated German bodies floating down the Rhine. I thought perhaps you might know him, though you rarely spoke of those days, and when you did only generally and vaguely as if the words were lodged deep within, buried for forty years, and no occasion right for the prying. Except for that one summer afternoon when you opened up to me on the front porch, told me secrets only hinted at through the years.

Early March, 1945. You are a 22-year-old staff sergeant from Pennsylvania. The day before reaching the bridge you volunteer to gather the remains of a friend who stepped on a land mine, wrap into your gray wool army issue blanket the unrecognizable remains of a 21-year-old Kentucky boy. And later that night, you sleep in the cellar of a bombed out farmhouse, only to awaken to melting snow piles: make-shift deep freezers for rotting German soldiers left behind by their hasty comrades.

When your battalion reaches the Ludendorff Bridge at Remagen the next day, the howling German guns firing from across the river greet you. The next morning you awaken to the spit and crackle of plane engines the German sent to bomb the bridge. Three planes fly low, buzzing the bridge, you said, and two of them, after missing the bridge with their bombs, are blown from the sky by artillery. The third plane flies loops and circles until climbing for the sun, a wing on fire, explodes, the pilot bailing out, his parachute blossoming like a seed blown from a pod of milkweed by the wind, gliding toward the earth. You sight him in your rifle scope, but rather than pull the trigger, find yourself amused by his airy ballet. "I knew he'd never make the ground alive, Geneva Conventions notwithstanding," you said. "I didn't have to be the one to shoot him." The Germans sent V-2 rockets which killed three of their own men and a few cows in a nearby pasture. And that afternoon, a whole army of Germans gladly surrendered to a handful of surprised American soldiers who happened upon them. Later, the message came that Eisenhower cheered your battalion's taking the bridge.

Marching with the first troops across the Rhine that spring into the Ruhr Valley to capture Mannheim and Nuremburg, you made it all the way to the Elbe River and on to Torgau, where tired, hungry Russians greeted you with great handshakes and hugs, while in the nearby Birnback Cemetery four German soldiers took the fall for losing the bridge—shot in the back of the head on Hitler's orders.

And so, forty years later, I search for you among the tired faces in the old newsreels, watch the camera shake as it always does when the bombs fall, watch the same bodies being pulled from the same rubble when the bridge finally collapses. I look for the soldier coming across the bridge in rain and fog, the one stopping along the road to Mannheim to remove a swastika from the arm of a 12 year old boy—armbands Hitler thought would make small boys soldiers. I search for the young man looking down into the open eyes of a German boy who stares back for forty years, and know why I won't send you this clipping celebrating this victory.

BROTHERS: GRIEF AND HAPPINESS

My brothers—one named for the great Venetian traveler,
and the other for our grandfather who passed through
the Great Hall at Ellis Island with the name
"Umberto" pinned to his chest—work in a chemical plant
my oldest brother tried to organize back in '68 but lost
by eight votes. That means they now work in an open shop;
that they have the right to work, the right to spit blood,
the right to have nose bleeds and wheeze when they cough.

Brothers, do you remember the smell of our father's breath
when he returned home from the night shift at the conveyor
factory, then came to our rooms where we were sleeping,
bent down to kiss us good night: blend of flesh, grease, blue J. C.
Penny Big Mac chambray work shirt, Pall Mall smoke, exhaustion?
Was this his blessing bestowed upon us for the life to come?

Brothers, I pray that your lungs gush red; that your bones
rattle clean and white, strong as piano keys; that you cough
hearty and loud into your eighties; that you know the way
it is during my once-a-year visit is the way it always
was for me, and is the way I'll always remember it.
Brothers, I pray that your houses are quiet at night;
that the only sound is the sound of your children's chests
rising and falling in the darkness of their sleep;
and that you always remember to give them the father's blessing:
fleshy, greasy, smoky.

And even if we spit blood and our noses bleed,
if we get only a little happiness from this life,
it's OK because a little grief goes a long way.
But a little happiness stays with us a lifetime.

ISAAC'S LAMENT

"And Abraham stretched forth his hand and took the knife to slay his son." GEN. 22:10

From the day I sprouted from the barren womb,
my name bore my mother's doubts about my birth,
mocking the core of my existence. Had she known
about my days to follow, she would have lived out
her barren days or delivered her own life to the
makeshift altar, rather than see her own son offered.

To this day, my hundred and eighty years, my wealth,
my power, my blessings, I would gladly offer just
to hear my father's refusal to bind my feet, to lay
me down upon a rickety altar before God, to hear him
from the deep cavern of his throat shout heavenward:
"This is my son come forth from the barren womb and
I will not offer him to you so willingly this day!"

What did I know that morning when my father came
to me, bid me gather fire wood and ready myself
for the journey? Where was the ram that day?
You, you who have your miracle wine at Cana,
your supper and broken Eucharist,
your Resurrection to rejoice in—
I carried wood to my own sacrifice,
while my own father carried the firestone and blade,
the one he would use against my throat.
I was the ram carrying my own sacrificial wood.

Do you think in all these years,
these endless nights,
that I haven't been over the arguments?
That my long life has not been curse to me?
Maybe it proves a human's love for his maker,
that it pushes devotion to its end.
But where does devotion stop?
Where in the terrible obedience do I fit in?
That his hand did not come down upon me
gives me no comfort. He may as well have slit
the veins in my throat, for all I care.
Had I been struck down the next day

by a wild ass would have pleased me more
than to live with his hand above me.

What father walks willingly as executioner
to his own son's death? What father offers
his own son as devotion and gift?
Only a God does that, not an ordinary man.
Perhaps now you will understand my weakness,
why, in my blindness, I blessed my undeserving son.
I have been the ram in the thicket of my years.

I hope that you never feel the weight
of your own sacrificial wood, the ties binding
your ankles and wrists in the afternoon sun.
Pray that you never see your father's hand
raised against you, against a blue sky,
that your eyes never have to gaze into his
then turn away into the glint of the knife's blade.

THE HAPPY ITALIAN

Masaccio, Sloppy Tom, was Vasari right?
Is painting nothing more than things as they are?
Were the sad faces of the Madonnas and saints
of childhood put there to tell us something of the life to come?
Day after day, we stared up at their faces staring down at us.
Was this ecstasy? Was this the way of the world?
Who carved those bodies, innocent as all nakedness?
Who painted those smileless and joyless faces?
Who rendered in oil, flesh smooth as marble, the Madonnas,
And the great saints, pale and sober as Old Testament prophets?
How sad we must have looked in the joy of our ordinary lives!

I looked for him in Bellini's "St. Francis in Ecstasy,"
but in all his mystic rapture I saw bewilderment:
sad-faced Francis, barefoot before God,
stone-faced ecstasy, cold and hard
as the giant cliffs around him.
In the presence of God, Bellini,
even your perfect Madonna seemed reluctant,
the child struggling to get away.
I looked for vigor and strength,
but smiling was not popular back then.
I looked for the happy Italian but could not find him.

Tiziano Vecellio, in her golden radiance
your Virgin seemed puzzled and timid
in her finest moment, her glorious
Assumption into Heaven.
Raphael Sanzio, I looked for him
in your most famous of all "Sistine Madonna"
but found only wide-eyed fright in the young child
and the not-so-sure mother and putti.

Lorenzo Lotto, your sad-faced Madonna and child
made all the saints unhappy. What were they seeing
in their glorious moment? Dominico Veneziano,
your "Madonna and Child with Saints" also wore
the faces of sadness. In their sacred conversation,
what were they whispering to each other day after day?
Was it something sad the world was never to know?

Years later, I remembered all these looks
in the faces of old Italian women when, as a child,
I held the paten to catch the falling Host.
I saw it in the eyes of the joyless priests
who taught us life was suffering and pain,
that a sinner's heart was a flower choked by weeds.
I remembered the look in the sullen faces
of holy factory workers coming from the graveyard shift.
I remember it in my father's eyes and my mother's face
when they greeted each other after work on Factory Avenue.

So what about ordinary happiness?
Give it up for the next life? Wait around?
What's left for us little ones?
In the eyes of the faithful,
is sadness triumph? Sorrow, glory?
No. That's not enough for me.
I'll look for him in my own face.
I'll look for him in my own heart.
In the ecstasy of this world,
I'll find the happy Italian.

FISHING WITH MY FATHER

Father, back then I always dreamed it this way:
when I got home from school you would be in the basement,
readying your tackle box, everything in its right place—
jigs, spinners, brass spoons, sinkers, bobbers.
And all those frightening lures with magical names:
Sassy Shad, Heddon Torpedo and Zara Spook.

Hearing me, you'd call "Son, let's go fishing," then rise
from the basement in your chamois shirt and angler vest,
khaki pants with filet knife tight in its holder against the belt.
Bean fisherman shoes. And that beautiful hat, slightly tilted
to the left, pinned with a blue and scarlet fly you so perfectly tied.
You'd carry the rods until we were outside, then hand
me mine in a gesture so fine I knew we were best friends.

Out at Lost Lake you were master:
you knew the depths, when to change rigs, when the fish
were moving, how to give out just the right length of line
before setting the hook, firm and tight into the boney lip.
And then the landing—nothing ever escaped your hold.

Driving home in evening twilight, we'd talk baseball,
the split willow creel always full, the fish sleeping
in their bed of cool moss and ferns.
At home, your knife—always holding its edge—
was quick and clean through the bloody gills.
You knew just how to do it, saving all that flesh
that later would taste so firm and sweet
cooked your secret way.

But none of this ever happened.
It was just a dream I carried with me all those days.
It was to be for other sons and fathers.

Last night, twenty-two years and a thousand miles away,
I dreamt of you again. It was dusk. I was on Lost Lake,
just off the shoreline drifting toward the deep trenches.
Then I saw you standing on the shoreline.
You started walking toward me, carrying this stringer
so thick and heavy with fish,
fresh and sweet as all the love in the world.
Father, forgive me that other dream.
What I saw as weakness then was so much strength.

ON FACTORY AVENUE

When we reach the stop sign near his old mill on Factory Avenue, my father glances toward the gate house and, as if on cue, begins telling me how he loved walking through those gates when the 3 o'clock whistle blew and punching his time card. In the parking lot you'd hear guys happy to be done with work, he tells me, guys yelling at each other and doors slamming and engines starting and dirt and gravel flying all over the place. He points toward old man Cioffi's place and tells me how he'd head toward George's Market on 12th Street, sometimes stopping off at the European Bakery on 11th and buying a fresh loaf of Vienna bread for supper. As I pull away from the stop sign, he's mapping out all of this to me with the sweep of his arm, hand and finger, carving an invisible route in the air because the mill's been closed for nearly twenty years, the gate house and parking lot empty, there's no more European Bakery or George's Market, and strangers live in Cioffi's place. It's as though he's still back there, listening to something far off and long ago, conducting he music of his life on Factory Avenue.

I hear longing in his voice as it trails off to the present. It's the real world symphony, the 3 o'clock steam whistle howling at him as he turns away from all that and asks me if I remember the night—a few months after the mill shut down and he lost his job after thirty-one years—I found him collapsed on the bathroom floor, his stomach ruptured in ulcers. He asks me if I remember. And I do.

We turn off Factory Avenue onto the highway and head for the airport so I can catch a plane for home. He's listening to a music only he can hear. Something none of us can imagine. How easily life is diminished. How difficult it must be to turn away from the beautiful music of America.

TWO PHOTOGRAPHS OF MY FATHER

1.

It is France, circa 1945.
You have spent the last few days
speeding across Europe in a Citroën.
The French woman sitting next to you,
arms wrapped around your neck like a scarf,
will never be my mother.

R & R: the Riviera.
You step toward me, fatigued,
your black hair swept across your head.
Behind you, three men stoop over
a card table near a gray sea
that is still and foreign.
Closer, I see
your father's thin gold watch chain
swinging from your hip.
He knew it would bring you home.

2.

Grandfather:
this is how I remember him.
Sitting up in bed, leaning
against a wooden headboard
grandmother at his side
holding a cigarette to his lips.
It was the emphysema
that killed him two days later.

In the background
you lean out of focus,
your mouth speaking
a blur of words.
Your father's eyes
come to meet yours
before they close.
Behind you, the wallpaper,
a sea of flowers,
death gurgling in his lungs.

GO FIGURE

I'm on the Indianapolis-to-Pittsburgh night shuttle. Thirty-thousand feet below, the fields of Ohio and then the lights along the riverbanks of the Ohio, as the pilot announces the beginning of our descent into Pittsburgh, where my father lies in a hospital bed, being readied for tomorrow's surgery. His ureter, bladder, urethra and prostate will be removed because their cells have gone awry, like a Fourth-of-July bottle rocket-turned-sidewinder spinning across the night. Somehow all I can think of is the tag line repeated by a comedian last night on TV. "Go figure," he'd say after asking some ambiguous or impenetrable question or posing an imponderable premise. "Go figure," he'd say, shrugging his shoulders in consternation.

After driving into the city, speeding down the Parkway and out of the Ft. Pitt Tunnel to the glorious city of lights along the rivers, I get to the hospital just in time to kiss him on the cheek, tell him that I love him, that I'll be staying as long as I'm needed. I'll try to sleep and return early the next morning for pre-op when we'll all be told what to expect. What to hope for. I remember the conversation I had a four years ago when the family doctor, who must have thought of me as if I were still a child, explained the male urinary system to me by drawing a line diagram with his gold Cross pen on a prescription pad. I wanted to tell him "I *know* all about the male urinary tract. Tell me something I don't know."

The next morning when we get to my father's hospital room we're told everything's going well, ahead of schedule. His surgeon meets with us and explains the operation in detail but warns that they may find other complications once they're inside. Things are sometimes worse than they appear. "We have a crack surgical team," he says. "Give us eight hours." But there's no guarantee. Eight hours. I think how it all comes down to this. Say you're lucky for fifty-nine years and then eight hours and it's a different life, buddy. All those other years gone, out the window, because it's all ahead of you now. A skilled surgeon will construct a new route to and through your stomach for your piss to travel, and it will, drop-by-drop, and your penis will be forever useless for that task. Just like that.

And just like that, eight hours later, he's back, a hole carved in his stomach where his piss is flowing, drop-by-drop, into a tube connected to a plastic pouch on the side of his bed.

A few days later when he is awake and talking and feeling alive, my father asks me to shave and wash him, so I lather his face and scrape the stubble from his cheeks and neck, then take a warm, white wash cloth to his body: neck, shoulders, arms, wrists, hands, chest. My father says go ahead, and lifts the gown to show me his stomach, swollen purple from above his navel to his groin and under to his rectum, held together with metal staples like an oversized zipper. My father points to his black and blue penis, shriveled and dangling, and asks me what good is it anymore? I cannot give him an answer, but instead think of the first time I saw it when I stepped into the shower with him in 1957, when his thirty-four year old body was sleek and taut as a race horse, his muscles rippling along his stomach, and I watched him lather his neck and shoulders and arms and chest and legs, and his thick, long penis and balls swayed like a fleshy clapper against the bell of his thighs, and I looked embarrassingly to my own hairless six-year-old groin, shamed and confused by what I did not understand and was yet to be. And now twenty-four years later all that is gracefully carved away by a surgeon. Eight hours. A lifetime in the snap of the finger.

I think of the surgeon, my father's black and blue penis, the comedian. Who could invent those burning cells gone awry inside my father? How pain is like God: great and hurting and incomprehensible. How all those days and months and years are rendered irrelevant by the careful hands of a surgeon, and even God is no longer there with you and you stand small and naked, confused and abandoned, the world an impenetrable dark, and all you have in place of understanding is human love, the kind that is given to you. Go figure.

67

LIGHTING A CANDLE FOR MY MOTHER AND FATHER
AT CHARTRES CATHEDRAL

*"And yet there is someone, whose hands
infinitely calm, hold up this falling."* —Rilke

If you were here, you would do the same for me: drop a coin in
the metal offering box, light your candle with the flame from
another, then offer me a prayer. But who receives the prayer of
the doubter? Perhaps this wall, thick and blackened with the
soot and smoke of candles for a hundred years? Or is this where
grief and sorrow go when they leave the hearts of the ones for
whom these candles were lit?

Sometimes, walking home at dusk, I'll notice a light going on in
the room of a house along the street where I now live and
remember the child from those awkward years when he was lost
in the world. How, climbing the hill toward home, he would
steady his body against the cold, fix his eyes on the light in the
window and pray he would not die before reaching the only
place he ever wanted to be.

The architect designs a space where we can find our way
through the labyrinth of grief to the holy place. Your light was
the gift I followed. Today, lighting this candle, I whisper your
names.

A PHOTOGRAPH OF YOU AT THE HOUSE OF THE DEAD IN ASCONA

—for Sheila

Far from our village on the other side of the hill, we found the holy chancel of the Madonna della Fontana. We made offerings, lit candles, rested in the shade of olive trees from the afternoon heat. Later, we found a short cut to our village, a steep stone path our map said would bring us there in half the distance than the road that brought us here. And it did.

Halfway down the hill, we found an abandoned chapel. The wooden doors were faded and shut tight with a rusty chain and lock. But through the window bars we counted six pews and a few broken chairs; saw red shards of votive candles scattered on a stone floor; smelled mildew and rotting boards and dank stone. And against the altar, two crutches and metal leg braces stood, relics of a fortunate pilgrim.

Carved in stone above the doorway, a skull and crossbones and the words *La Casa della Morte*—the House of the Dead, where the living come to pray. There in mid-July heat and haze, far above Lake Maggiore, we paused in our journey down to the village, and I photographed you sitting on the steps of the House of the Dead.

That night, long before the piazza cafés fell silent, we fell into bed, exhausted from our pilgrimage. Later, we were awakened by the sweet voice of an Italian tenor singing arias in the hotel lobby three floors below, his voice floating like an angel in the cool Swiss night, rising to our open window, then drifting above the village rooftops beyond the bell tower of Santi Pietro e Paolo, into the hillsides. And we turned to each other, certain we were not dreaming the same dream, remembering our afternoon searching for the Madonna of the Fountain, descending the steep stone path, pausing at the House of the Dead, so full of life and love.

WALKING THE CLOISTER AT NEW COLLEGE, OXFORD, LISTENING TO THE CHOIR REHEARSING BACH'S "MAGNIFICAT"

Late afternoon. Light fading. Air damp and chilled. We are among friends, and each step we take falls upon smooth stone where choir songs have risen for six hundred years, praising the Lord of stone and light! Today the voices we come upon praise the one who gave praise. A child moves toward its mother in the tunnel with many windows, and the distance between them diminishes. We think each step carries us closer to the voice inside, but the voice is seeking us.

There is a quietness among friends who walk together on smooth stone. With whom do we travel down the corridor of hosts when the holy one we walk with does not answer to the name of Jesus, Mary, Guardian Angel, Friend or The-One-We-Love?

LEAVES UNDER SNOW

Shoveling a path of newly fallen snow from the fence gate to the bird feeders, I scrape the edges of the lawn and uncover leaves forgotten and not raked in late autumn. Soft and wet, they are the color of chestnut mares caught in rain or the old leather pouches used to carry mail.

Hidden but not forgotten. They are like old friends I haven't called or written for a year. The ones I think about each day then lose in the busyness of this world. What I have not done. What I have set aside. A promise that flutters to the edge of the day then is veiled in white intention, like trees not seen across a field when fog settles in early morning, or the body of Christ wrapped in linen and placed in the new tomb at dusk.

WALKING TO MY OFFICE ON EASTER SUNDAY MORNING

I move through the quiet morning, watching
a cluster of blackbirds arc and dive above me,
vapor trails of jets, and below me the brown
grass and soggy trash revealed by melting snow.
New buds and a few white petals on an almond tree.
Passing Our Redeemer Church, I read the marquee,
usually filled with times for daily worship
and a quotation from scripture,
but today it says only "His work is done!"

Then the end of a hymn being sung
and the final notes of the organ rising.
And the congregation pouring out
in all their joy and the children
in their Easter pastels, colors we see
when we close our eyes and imagine light.
How we long to be lifted, carried from
this world by the spiraling energy
of the Psalms and wrapped in brilliant colors!
Colors I long ago put away.

Arriving at my office building,
I open the door left unlocked all night,
walk down the long hall to my office.
Sliding the key inside the brass knob,
I open the door to the dark and empty room.
Something inside of me rising.
No one to greet us on the long road.
So much work to be done.

A CHURCH IN ITALY

Last summer, in a church in Italy,
    I prayed for all of you: asked not for forgiveness
        and strength, but that all the sadness of our days,

all the grief of our lives,
    all the loneliness given us be taken away
        without judgment—asked for life and light.

That was the first time in twenty-three years something
    like that happened to me. Not knowing the modern prayers,
        I fell back on the old way of ending prayer, recited:

Glory be to the Father and to the Son
    and to the Holy Spirit, as it was in the beginning,
        is now, and ever shall be, world without end

then dropped some lire coins in the metal offering box,
    walked through the heavily curtained doorway into the
        Mediterranean heat, into the hard traffic of the village,
            into the harsh light of the afternoon,
                into this world without end.

FISHING THE LAKE

—for Bob Carothers

Young in our beards,
we are like old Italians
fishing the lake at dawn.

Near the boat, fish break
beautifully arching themselves,
their bellies blossom in light.
Soon they will dive deep,
twist and curl beneath the water,
to cool themselves.

While you row,
I hold on for dear life:

we are between a hundred-thousand ripples.

ABOUT THE AUTHOR

Thom Tammaro, the grandson of Italian immigrants, was born and raised in the heart of the steel valley of western Pennsylvania. He has lived and worked in Pennsylvania, Kansas, Indiana and, since 1983, in Moorhead, Minnesota, where he is Professor of Multidisciplinary Studies at Moorhead State University.

His poems, essays and reviews have appeared in numerous anthologies and magazines, including *After the Storm: Poems on the Persian Gulf War; Beyond Borders: An Anthology of New Writing from Manitoba, Minnesota, Saskatchewan, and the Dakotas; Bless Me, Father: Stories of Catholic Childhood; Two Worlds Walking: Writers with Mixed Heritages* and *Chicago Review, College Composition and Communication, Midwest Quarterly, North Dakota Quarterly, Quarterly West, South Dakota Review* and *The Sun: A Magazine of Ideas.* His chapbook of poems, *Minnesota Suite,* was published by Spoon River Poetry Press in 1987.

He has co-edited *Imagining Home: Writing from the Midwest* (University of Minnesota Press, 1995); *Inheriting the Land: Contemporary Voices from the Midwest* (University of Minnesota Press, 1993), an anthology of poetry, short fiction and essays and winner of a 1994 Minnesota Book Award. He has also edited *Roving Across Fields: A Conversation with William Stafford and Uncollected Poems.*

ACKNOWLEDGMENTS

My sincere thanks to the editors of the following magazines where these poems first appeared, sometimes in different forms:

Crazy River: A Journal of the Midwest: "Route 65"; *The Flying Island:* "On Factory Avenue"; *Great River Review:* "Dancing With Susie" and "Prayer for the Conversion of Russia"; *Indianapolis Inprint:* "Fishing the Lake" and "Two Photographs of My Father"; *The Mill Hunk Herald:* "Brothers: Grief and Happiness"; *North Dakota Quarterly:* "Eternity," "February, 1951," "Innocent Traveler," "Pausing Under a Streetlight," "Story Problems" and "Union Meeting, 1959"; *The Pittsburgh Quarterly:* "On Being Asked If There Was Art and Culture In the Town Where I Grew Up"; *Sidewalks:* "Looking for My Father at the Remagen Bridge" and "Remembering Bull DeLisio"; *South Dakota Review:* "Grandmother's Song," "Isaac's Lament" and "St. Peter's Tears"; *The Sun: A Magazine of Ideas:* "Go Figure," "Leaves Under Snow" and "Walking to My Office on Easter Sunday Morning"; *University of Windsor Review:* "A Church in Italy," "Fishing With My Father" and "A Photograph of You at the House of the Dead in Ascona."

"Fishing With My Father" appeared in the chapbook *Minnesota Suite* (Granite Falls, Minnesota: Spoon River PoetryPress, 1987).

"The Happy Italian" appeared in the anthology *The Heartlands Today: A Cultural Quilt.* Huron, OH: Firelands Writing Center, 1992.

"A Photograph of You at the House of the Dead in Ascona" also appeared in *Beyond Borders: An Anthology of New Writing from Manitoba, Minnesota, Saskatchewan and the Dakotas.* Winnipeg: Turnstone Press & Minneapolis: New Rivers Press, 1992.

"St. Peter's Tears" received the 1987 *South Dakota Review* Poetry Award.

"The Woman Who Cured Fits": I first heard several versions of this story when I was growing up in western Pennsylvania during the 1950s. Years later, I read a version of the story in *Flatlanders and Ridgerunners: Folktales from the Mountains of Northern Pennsylvania*, edited by James York Grimm. University of Pittsburgh Press, 1983.

"Workers": excerpts from *Out of This Furnace: A Novel of Immigrant Labor in America* by Thomas Bell. NY: Little, Brown and Company, 1941. Rpt. University of Pittsburgh Press, 1976.

I wish to express my gratitude to Moorhead State University for a Release Time Award, to the Minnesota State Arts Board for a Fellowship in Poetry, and to The Loft and the McKnight Foundation for a Loft-McKnight Award, all of which provided time and support during the completion of this book. I am also grateful for the unwavering friendships of Sheila Coghill, Jay Meek, Tom Koontz and Mark Vinz.